Lullabies

AN ILLUSTRATED SONGBOOK

MUSIC ARRANGED BY RICHARD KAPP

THE METROPOLITAN MUSEUM OF ART
NEW YORK

Gulliver Books
Harcourt Brace & Company

San Diego   New York   London

Front jacket and cover: *Maternal Caress.* Mary Cassatt, American, 1844–1926.
Drypoint, aquatint, and soft-ground etching, printed in color; 1890–91.
Gift of Paul J. Sachs, 1916   16.2.5.

Back jacket and cover: *Jonathan.* Eliot Porter, American, 1901–1990.
Gelatin silver print, 1938. Alfred Stieglitz Collection, 1949   49.55.287.
© 1990, Amon Carter Museum, Fort Worth, Texas, Bequest of Eliot Porter.

Back jacket flap: *Portrait of a Child (Clara B. Fuller).* Lucia Fairchild Fuller, American, 1872–1924.
Watercolor on ivory, 1898. Rogers Fund, 1914   14.57.3.

Page 1: *Sleeping.* Detail from *A Day in a Child's Life.* Hand-colored wood engraving after a drawing
by Kate Greenaway (British, 1846–1901), 1881. Rogers Fund, 1921   21.36.91.

Page 3: Illustration from *Vieilles chansons et rondes pour les petits enfants.* Maurice Boutet de Monvel,
French, 1851–1913. Published in Paris. Gift of Mrs. John S. Lamont, 1974   1974.669.

Pages 6–7: Illustrations from *Le Journal de Bébé* by Marie Madeleine Franc-Nohain. Published by Bernard
Grasset, Paris, 1914. The Elisha Whittelsey Collection, The Elisha Whittelsey Fund, 1977   1977.588.1.

Work by Romare Bearden, p. 29: Works of Romare Bearden are licensed by VAGA, New York, NY. Works by
Jean Charlot, pp. 31, 69: Reproduced with the permission of Mrs. Dorothy Zohmah Charlot and the Jean
Charlot Estate. Works by Pierre Bonnard, pp. 36, 39, 48: © 1997 Artists Rights Society (ARS), New
York/ADAGP, Paris. Work by Eliot Porter, p. 40 and back cover: © 1990, Amon Carter
Museum, Forth Worth, Texas, Bequest of Eliot Porter. Work by Alma Lavenson, p. 60:
Courtesy Alma Lavenson Associates and Susan Ehrens. Work by Henry Moore,
p. 76: Reproduced by permission of the Henry Moore Foundation.

Music for "Dance, Little Baby" and "Matthew, Mark,
Luke, and John" composed by Paul Kapp.

Published by The Metropolitan Museum of Art, New York, and Gulliver Books,
an imprint of Harcourt Brace & Company.

ISBN 0-87099-791-2 (MMA)
ISBN 0-15-201728-3 (Harcourt Brace)

Produced by the
Department of Special Publications,
The Metropolitan Museum of Art
Music arrangements by Richard Kapp
Photography on page 48 by Malcolm Varon, N.Y.
All other photography by The Metropolitan
Museum of Art Photograph Studio
Designed by Barbara Balch

Printed in Italy
First edition
A C E F D B

CONTENTS

Introduction   6

Hush, Little Baby   8

Dance to Your Daddy   10

Now the Day Is Over   12

All the Pretty Little Horses   14

Mammy Loves   17

Sleep, Baby, Sleep   18

Dance, Little Baby   20

Brahms' Lullaby   23

Armenian Lullaby   26

Swing Low, Sweet Chariot   28

Can Ye Sew Cushions   30

Mozart's Lullaby   34

The Sandman   37

Raisins and Almonds   38

All Through the Night   40

Golden Slumbers   44

Skidamarink   46

Day Is Done   49

Suo Gan (Lullaby)   50

By'm Bye   52

Rocking   54

Baby's Bed's a Silver Moon   56

Rock-a-Bye, Baby   60

Little Boy Blue   62

Baloo, Baleerie   64

Brezairola (Lullaby)   66

Kumbayah   70

Raindrops   72

Sweet and Low   74

Fais Dodo (Go to Sleep)   78

Toora, Loora, Loora   80

Bye, Baby Bunting   83

Twinkle, Twinkle, Little Star   84

When at Night I Go to Sleep   86

Matthew, Mark, Luke,
    and John   89

All Night, All Day   90

Good Night to You All   92

Index of Song Titles   94

Index of First Lines   95

Credits   96

INTRODUCTION

The time spent before going to sleep can be one of the sweetest pleasures children and grown-ups share. After the day's busy activities, bedtime is a chance to snuggle together, to recall the events of the day, to create an atmosphere of calm and quiet for the night. Music is often a part of this evening ritual, for lullabies provide a bridge between daytime and dreaming, as they soothe fears, express love, or inspire visions of delights. Gathered here are thirty-seven lullabies, some classic, some less familiar, and all illustrated with works of art from the collections of The Metropolitan Museum of Art.

These songs represent a wide variety of musical styles and traditions, ranging from lullabies by famous composers and poets to simple, anonymous folk songs. Many have a lilting rhythm that mimics a rocking motion. Others have a gentle, murmuring tone that encourages slumber. Also included are livelier songs, for when a child awakens or for babies who respond to music with a definite beat, and a few songs that children can sing to themselves.

The lyrics of these lullabies calm and comfort, some with pleasant imagery of toys and treats, some with reassurances of the parents' love and protection, some with prayers of safekeeping. Of course, tiny babies can't understand the words, anyway, and some of

the most effective songs are composed of soothing nonsense syllables: "toora, loora, loora," or "baloo, baleerie."

The songs originated in the British Isles, the American South, Eastern Europe, and other places around the world. The works of art that accompany them similarly come from a wide variety of cultures and times. An ancient Greek sculpture, a Victorian painting, and a twentieth-century photograph all celebrate the innocent contentment of sleep. The tender communication between mothers and children is captured in Mary Cassatt's touching portraits and Gertrude Käsebier's thoughtful photographs, as well as in sculptures from Oceania and ancient Egypt. Views of the family can be found in prints by Pierre Bonnard and Kitagawa Utamaro and a sculpture by Henry Moore. And some of the timeless tools for comforting children are represented by an English seventeenth-century cradle, a Shaker rocking chair, and a Colonial American rattle. Moonlit landscapes, watchful angels, and scenes of nature at rest further evoke tranquillity and quiet.

The songs induce sleepiness, and the images reflect the tenderness and affection that grown-ups feel as they gaze at their now-slumbering children. With soft lashes, dewy cheeks, and damp curls, is there anything sweeter than a sleeping child?

Carolyn Vaughan, Editor

Hush, Little Baby

This catalogue of gifts—
and Papa's endless willingness
to replace broken toys—has
delighted babies over the years.

Rocking

1. Hush, lit-tle ba-by, don't say a word, Pa-pa's gon-na buy you a
(2.) if that__ dia-mond ring turns to brass, Pa-pa's gon-na buy you a
(3.) if that__ bil-ly goat don't__ pull, Pa-pa's gon-na buy you a
(4.) if that__ dog named Rover don't__ bark, Pa-pa's gon-na buy you a

mock-ing-bird. And if that mock-ing- bird don't sing,
look-ing glass. And if that look-ing glass gets broke,
cart and bull. And if that cart and bull turn over,
horse and cart. And if that horse and cart fall down, You'll

for more verses

Pa-pa's gon-na buy you a dia-mond ring. 2. And
Pa-pa's gon-na buy you a bil-ly goat. 3. And
Pa-pa's gon-na buy you a dog named Rover. 4. And

The Hatch Family
Eastman Johnson
American, 1824–1906
Oil on canvas, 1870–71

still be the sweet - est lit - tle ba - by in town.

First Steps, after Millet
Vincent van Gogh
Dutch, 1853–1890
Oil on canvas

Dance to Your Daddy

Gently swinging

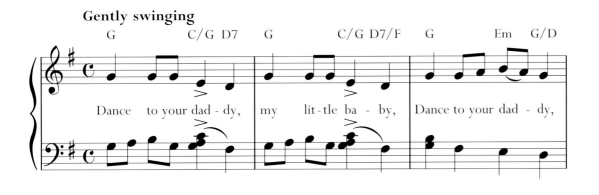

Dance to your dad - dy, my lit - tle ba - by, Dance to your dad - dy,

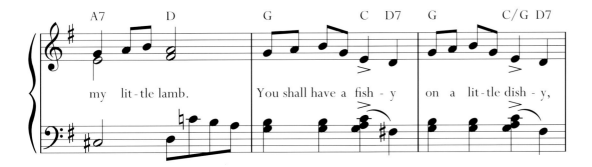

my lit - tle lamb. You shall have a fish - y on a lit - tle dish - y,

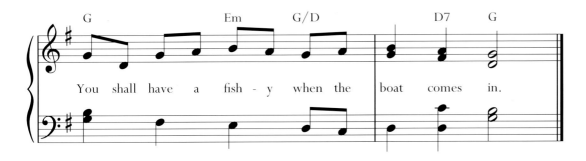

You shall have a fish - y when the boat comes in.

Based on a Scottish dandling rhyme, this song became popular in communities where men were often at sea and women comforted their children and themselves with thoughts of the boats' return.

Madame Roulin and Her Baby
Vincent van Gogh
Dutch, 1853–1890
Oil on canvas

Now the Day Is Over

This gentle hymn evokes the calm that settles over the land, and the household, as night descends. Lyrics by the Reverend Sabine Baring-Gould (1834–1924) were set to music by Sir Joseph Barnby (1838–1896).

A Domestic Scene
Annibale Carracci
Italian, 1560–1609
Pen and black ink, gray
and brown wash;
early 1580s

Peacefully

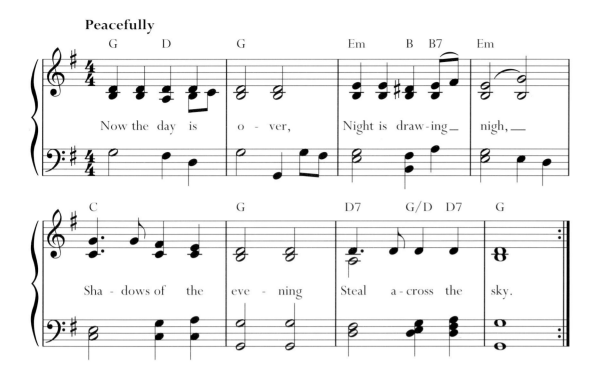

Now the day is o - ver,
Night is draw-ing nigh,

Sha - dows of the eve - ning
Steal a - cross the sky.

Gobelle's Mill at Optevoz
Charles-François Daubigny
French, 1817–1878
Oil on canvas

13

Mother and Child
Mary Cassatt
American, 1844—1926
Pastel on paper, ca. 1910

All the Pretty Little Horses

Originating in the American South, this lullaby has a haunting melody that soothes a child to sleep while its imagery inspires sweet dreams.

Robert Wade Young, Young Boy with Cock Horse
Augustin Edouart
British (b. France), 1789–1861
Cut-paper silhouette

(Please turn the page.)

All the Pretty Little Horses continued

José Costa y Bonnells, Called Pepito
Francisco de Goya
Spanish, 1746–1828
Oil on canvas

Children on a Rocking Horse (detail)
Josef von Divèky
Austrian, 1887–1951
Color lithograph published by the
Wiener Werkstätte, Vienna

When you wake, you shall have cake And all the pret-ty lit-tle hors — es.

Blacks and bays, dap-ples and grays, Coach and six — white — hors — es.

Mammy Loves

Mam - my loves and Pap-py loves, And Mam-my loves_ her ba - by.

Go to sleep-y, go to sleep, Go to sleep, you lit-tle ba - by.

Babies love repetition. You can sing this song over and over, changing to the names of grand-parents, brothers and sisters, aunts and uncles, baby-sitters, and everyone else who loves the baby.

Mr. and Mrs. Daniel Otis and Child
Joseph H. Davis, American, 1811–1865
Watercolor, gum arabic, and graphite
on off-white wove paper; 1834

Sleep, Baby, Sleep

*A very old German song, "Schlaf, Kindlein Schlaf," this melody
has been incorporated into compositions by Brahms and Wagner.*

Lamb (detail)
Josef von Divèky
Austrian, 1887–1951
Color lithograph published by the
Wiener Werkstätte, Vienna

Slowly

1. Sleep, ba-by, sleep, Your fa-ther tends the sheep, Your moth-er shakes the
2. Sleep, ba-by, sleep, Our cot-tage vale is deep, The lit - tle lamb is

dream-land tree, And from it fall sweet dreams for thee, Sleep, ba - by,
on   the green, With snow-y fleece so soft and clean, Sleep, ba - by,

Pastoral Scene
Detail of needlework upholstery
on the back of an easy chair
American (Newport, Rhode Island), 1758
Wool on linen

1.

sleep, Sleep, ba-by, sleep.
sleep,

Last time *D.C.*

Sleep, ba-by, sleep.

Dance, Little Baby

The "merry gay coral" in this nursery rhyme is a kind of rattle common in the eighteenth and nineteenth centuries. The bells jingle and the coral can be used for teething. Since ancient times, coral has been believed to protect children against evil.

Rattle, with Whistle, Coral, and Bells
Nicholas Roosevelt
American (New York), 1715–1769
Gold, coral

Mother and Child
Edward Steichen
American, 1879–1973
Direct carbon print, 1905

Easily

Dance, lit - tle ba - by, dance up high, Nev - er mind, ba - by,

moth - er is by; Crow and — ca - per, ca - per and crow,

There, lit - tle ba - by, there you go; Up to the ceil - ing,

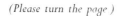

(Please turn the page)

20

Mother Playing with Children
Utagawa Toyoharu
Japanese, 1735–1806
Color on silk

Brahms' Lullaby

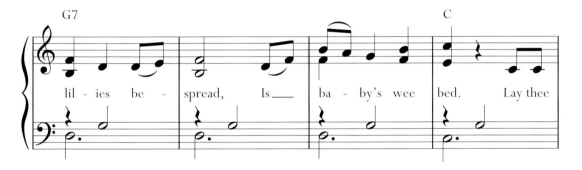

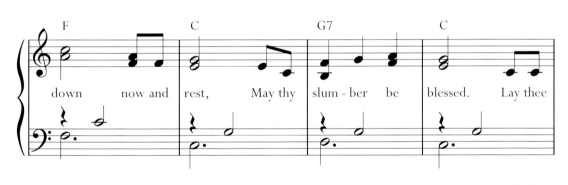

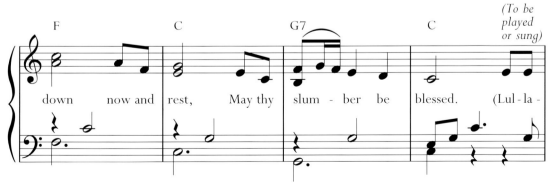

In this well-known lullaby by Johannes Brahms (1833–1897), the roses and lilies decorating baby's bed suggest the purity, innocence, and sweetness of the sleeping child.

(To be played or sung)

Infante Carlos Luis María Fernando de Borbón
Luis de la Cruz y Rios
Spanish, active by 1815, d. 1850
Ivory, 1818

(Please turn the page.)

Brahms' Lullaby continued

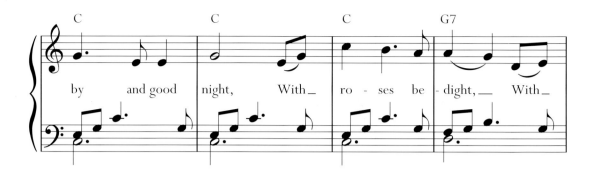

by and good night, With roses be-dight, With

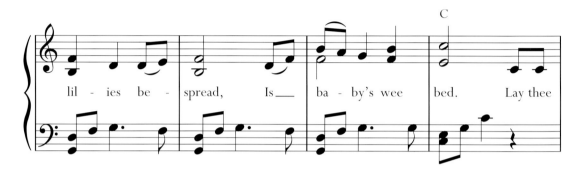

lil - ies be - spread, Is baby's wee bed. Lay thee

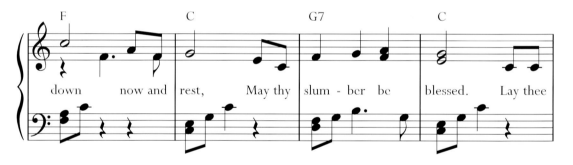

down now and rest, May thy slum - ber be blessed. Lay thee

Sleeping Eros
Greek, 3rd–2nd century B.C.
Bronze

24

Child Asleep (The Rosebud)
Thomas Sully
American, 1783–1872
Oil on canvas, 1841

down now and rest, May thy slum - ber be blessed.)

Armenian Lullaby

With its simple but beautiful melody in a minor key, this song has the feeling of an old, traditional folk tune.

Gently rocking

Sleep, my lit-tle one, my — loved one,

As I rock and sing, As the bright——

moon watch-es o'er us, O'er your lit - tle crib.

Peasant Mother and Child
Mary Cassatt
American, 1844–1926
Drypoint and aquatint printed in colors,
ca. 1894

Autumn Grasses (detail)
Shibata Zeshin
Japanese, 1807 1891
Panel from a two-fold screen;
ink, lacquer, and silver leaf on paper

Swing Low, Sweet Chariot

The words of this beloved spiritual express the thoughts of someone who is ready to lay down the cares of the world and to take heavenly rest.

Slow and lilting

Swing low, sweet char - i - ot, __ Com-in' for to car-ry me home.

Swing __ low, sweet char - i - ot, __ Com-in' for to car-ry me home. *Fine*

1. I looked o - ver Jor - dan and what did I see, ___
2. If you get to heav - en be - fore I do, ___

Com-in' for to car-ry me home, A band __ of an - gels
Com-in' for to car-ry me home, Tell all __ my friends I'm

com-in' af - ter me, __ Com-in' for to car-ry me home.
com-in' there, too, __ Com-in' for to car-ry me home.

The Block (detail)
Romare Bearden
American, 1911–1988
Cut-and-pasted papers
on Masonite, 1971

Shaker Rocking Chair
American, ca. 1820–50
Maple, birch

Can Ye Sew Cushions

The lyrics of this Scottish song seem gloomy, but the mother ("minnie")
is probably worrying about her children ("many o' ye, little for to gi' ye")
and trying to calm a baby who cries ("greets").

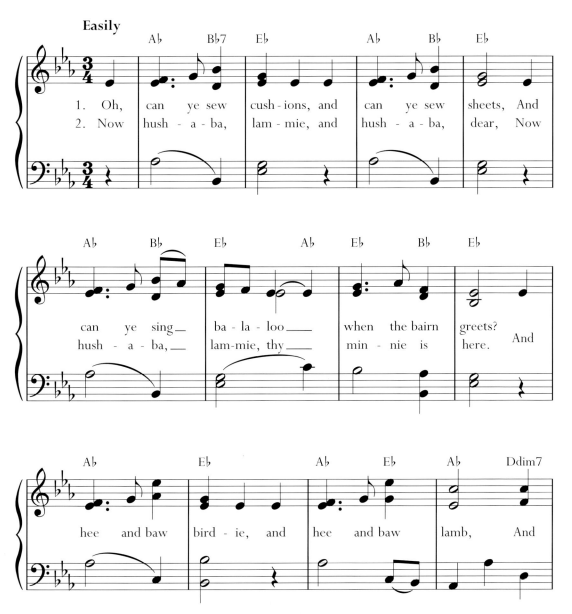

1. Oh, can ye sew cush-ions, and can ye sew sheets, And
2. Now hush - a - ba, lam - mie, and hush - a - ba, dear, Now

can ye sing___ ba - la - loo___ when the bairn greets? And
hush - a - ba,___ lam-mie, thy___ min - nie is here. And

hee and baw bird - ie, and hee and baw lamb, And

(Please turn the page.)

Rest and Work
Jean Charlot
Mexican, 1898–1979
Color lithograph on stone, 1945

Monday Morning
B. J. O. Norfeldt
American, 1878–1955
Color woodblock print

Penelope
Charles-François Marchal
French, 1825–1877
Oil on canvas

The Lacemaker
Nicolaes Maes
Dutch, 1634–1693
Oil on canvas

Mozart's Lullaby

Mozart's gentle harmonies seem a perfect accompaniment to these descriptions of nature at twilight.

Gently

Sleep, lit - tle one, go to sleep. So peace-ful the birds and the

sheep, Qui - et are mead-ow and trees,

The First Babe (detail)
Jehan-Georges Vibert
French, 1840–1902
Watercolor, 1872

Grand Piano
Ferdinand Hofmann (d. 1829)
Vienna, ca. 1790
Cherrywood and
other materials

E - ven the buzz of the bees, The sil - ver - y moon-beams so

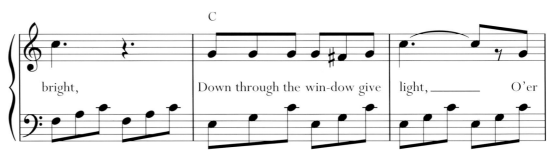

bright, Down through the win-dow give light,____ O'er

(Please turn the page.)

A Goose Hiding Its Head
Alfred Sisley
British, 1839–1899
Pencil and colored crayon on paper

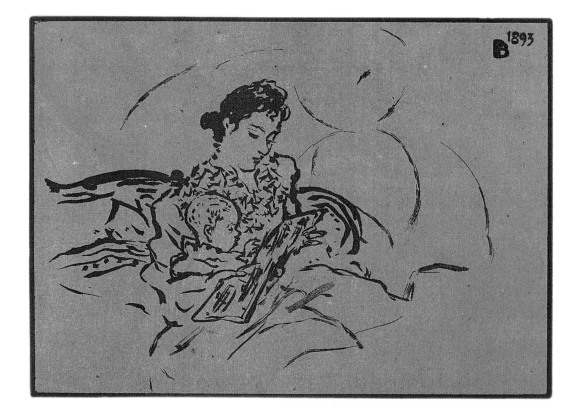

Mother and Child
Pierre Bonnard
French, 1867–1947
Lithograph; back cover of
Petit Solfège Illustré, 1893

The Sandman

The Sandman has made his way from folklore to popular culture as the benevolent being who sprinkles his sleep-inducing sand into children's eyes.

The Sand-man comes, The Sand-man comes. He brings such pret-ty snow-white sand, For ev-ery child through-out the land, The Sand-man comes.

Midnight: Mother and Sleepy Child
Kitagawa Utamaro
Japanese, 1753–1806
Polychrome woodblock print from the series *Customs of Women in the Twelve Hours*

Raisins and Almonds

The little goat in this Yiddish lullaby brings almonds and raisins, probably symbolizing the sweetness in life that parents wish for their children.

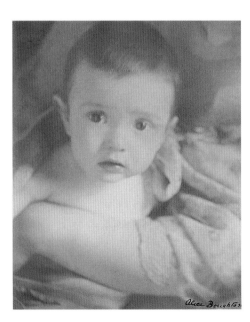

The Baby
Alice Boughton
American, 1865–1943
Gelatin silver print, 1908

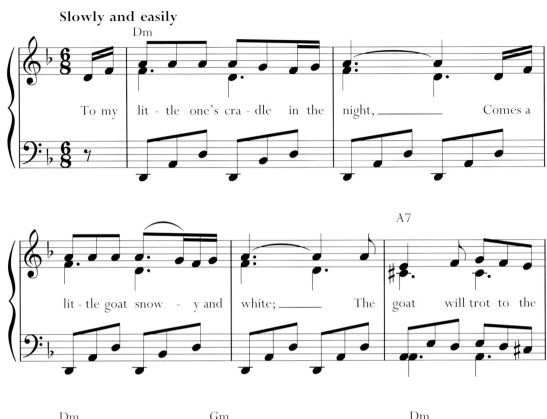

Slowly and easily

To my lit-tle one's cra-dle in the night,_____ Comes a

lit-tle goat snow——y and white;_____ The goat will trot to the

mar-ket,_____ While moth-er her watch_ does keep,

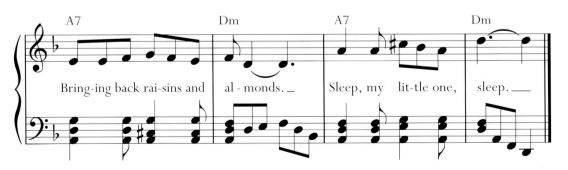

Bring-ing back rai-sins and al-monds._ Sleep, my lit-tle one, sleep.____

Village Scene
Pierre Bonnard
French, 1867–1947
Oil on canvas, 1912

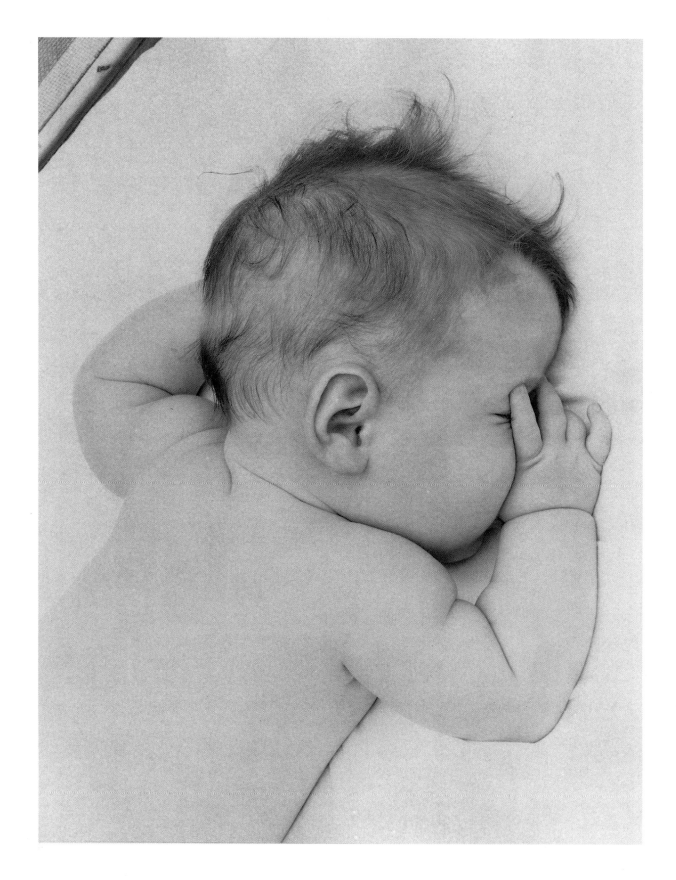

All Through the Night

*Set to a beautiful old Welsh folk tune, these lyrics by
Sir Harold Boulton (1859–1935) reassure children
that they are loved and protected, all through the night.*

Slowly

1. Sleep, my child, and peace at-tend thee, All through the night.
2. While the moon her watch is keep-ing, All through the night;

Guar-dian an-gels God will send thee, All through the night.
While the wea-ry world is sleep-ing, All through the night;

2nd time to ⊕

Soft the drow-sy hours are creep-ing, Hill and vale in slum-ber steep-ing,

Rabbit in a Landscape with Moon
Chinese, mid-18th century
Embroidered silk

Jonathan
Eliot Porter
American, 1901–1990
Gelatin silver print, 1938

(Please turn the page.)

*Bahram Gur Watching Dilaram Charm
the Wild Animals with Her Music*
Page from the *Hasht Behesht*
(Eight Paradises) of Amir Khusrau Dihlavi
Indian, Mughal, probably Lahore,
period of Akbar (r. 1556–1605)
Attributed to Miskin
Ink and opaque watercolor
on paper, ca. 1595

Mughal Virgin and Child
Indian, Mughal period, 17th century
Brush drawing, black and colored inks
and gold on paper

Golden Slumbers

Set to a seventeenth-century English tune, the lyrics of this lovely song are attributed to Thomas Dekker (1572–1632), the English dramatist. They are perhaps better known as sung by the Beatles.

Sleepily

1. Gol - den slum - bers kiss your eyes,
2. Care___ you know not, there - fore sleep,

Smiles___ a - wait you when you rise.
While___ I o'er you watch do keep.

Sleep, pret - ty ba - by, do___ not cry,___ And
Sleep, pret - ty dar - lings, do___ not cry,___ And

Cradle
English, first half of the 17th century
Oak and walnut

The Young Mother
Nicolaes Maes
Dutch, 1634–1693
Pen and brown ink, brown wash

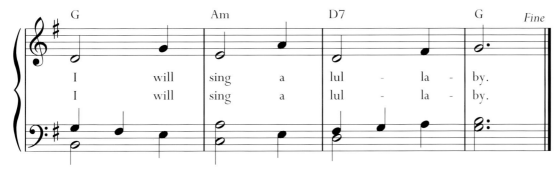

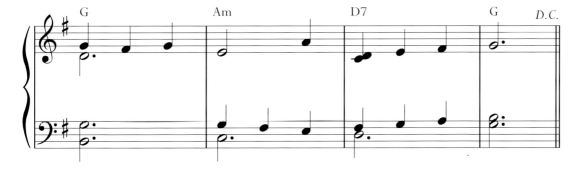

Lizzie at the Table
Fairfield Porter
American, 1907–1975
Oil on canvas, 1958

Skidamarink

Sing "Skidamarink" to a child waking up in the morning or after a nap,
or any time you want to say "I love you."

Lively enough

Skid-a-ma-rink a - dink a-dink, Skid-a-ma-rink a - doo,

I love you.

Skid-a-ma-rink a - dink a-dink, Skid-a-ma-rink a - doo,

I love you. I

(Please turn the page.)

Two Lovers, Sankatsu and
Hanhichi, with Their Baby
Kitagawa Utamaro
Japanese, 1753–1806
Polychrome woodblock print

Family Scene
Pierre Bonnard
French, 1867–1943
Color lithograph, 1893

Day Is Done

Very slowly—without a beat

p Day is done, Gone the sun, From the lake, From the hills, From the

sky. All is well, Safe - ly rest. God is nigh.

All the world is at peace and ready to rest at the end of the day.

Hooked Rug
Lucy Barnard
American (Dixfield Common, Maine)
Burlap, yarn, and cloth; ca. 1860

Suo Gan
(Lullaby)

*What could be more comforting
to a child than to be wrapped
in Mother's arms, snuggled
against her chest, as described
in this old Welsh song?*

Mother and Child
Mary Cassatt
American, 1844–1926
Pastel on wove paper, mounted on canvas,
1914

Easily and slowly

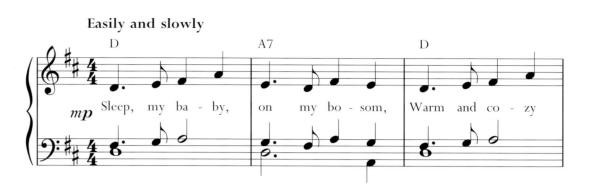

mp Sleep, my ba - by, on my bo - som, Warm and co - zy

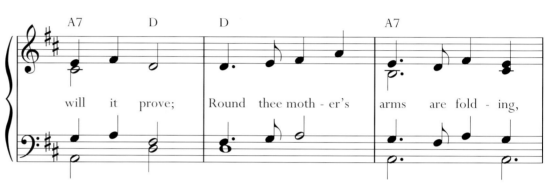

will it prove; Round thee moth - er's arms are fold - ing,

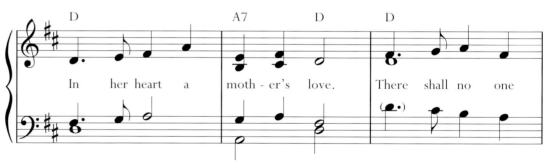

In her heart a moth - er's love. There shall no one

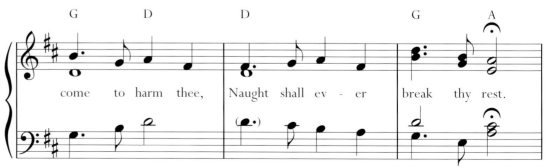

come to harm thee, Naught shall ev - er break thy rest.

Mother and Child
Camille Corot
French, 1796–1875
Oil on wood

Sleep, my dar-ling babe, in qui-et, Sleep on moth-er's gen-tle __ breast.

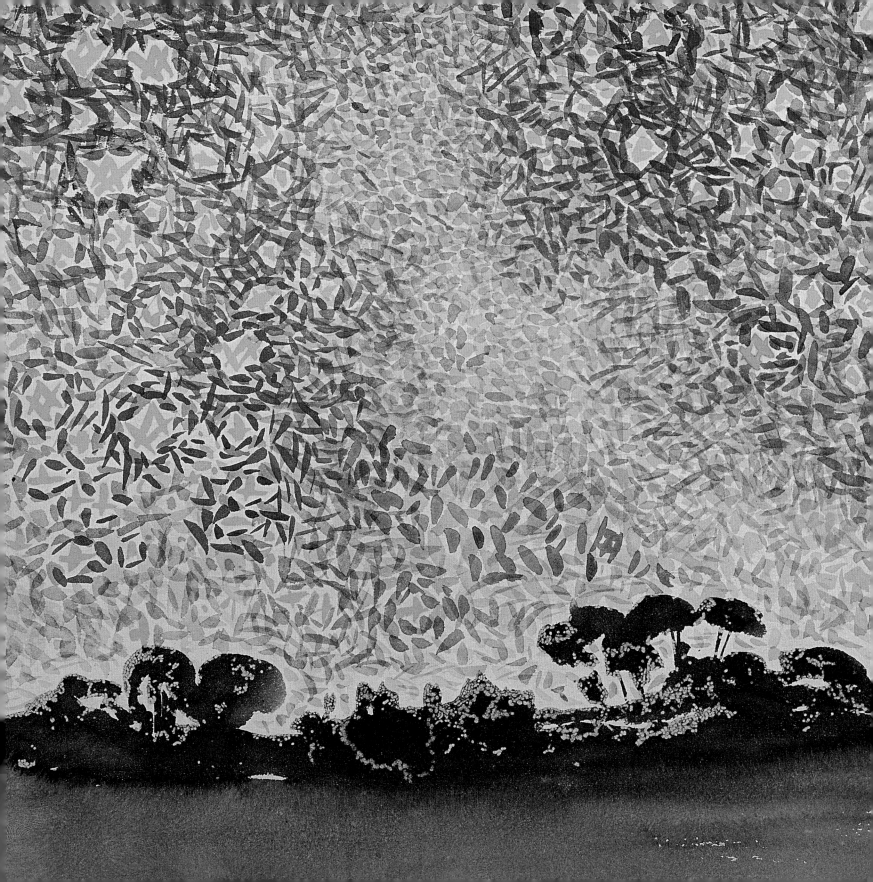

By'm Bye

Instead of counting sheep, try counting stars. You can continue
"Stars shining, number, number seven, number eight, number nine"
and so on until your child falls asleep.

Very freely

By'm bye, by'm bye, Stars shin - ing,

With a little movement

1. Num-ber, num-ber one, num-ber two, num-ber three, Good Lord, by'm
2. Num-ber, num-ber four, num-ber five, num-ber six, Good Lord, by'm

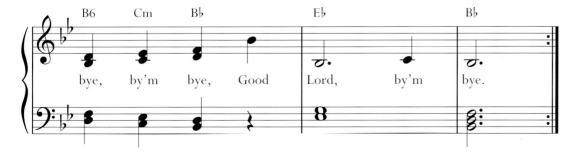

bye, by'm bye, Good Lord, by'm bye.

Alice Cushman
George Hewitt Cushman
American, 1814–1876
Watercolor on ivory, ca. 1856

Landscape with Stars (detail)
Henri-Edmond Cross
French, 1856–1910
Watercolor on paper

53

Rocking

A Czech carol, this song was originally a lullaby to the infant Jesus.

Standing Figure of Mother and Child
Oceania, Melanesia, Irian Jaya, Lake Sentani
region, Kabiterau village
Wood, 19th–20th century

*Young Mother
Nursing Her Baby*
Kitagawa Utamaro
Japanese, 1753–1806
Polychrome woodblock
print, 1790s

Baby's Bed's a Silver Moon

The vivid image of baby "sailing o'er the sea of sleep" is made poignant by the plea, "Only don't forget to come back again to me."

Imaginary Voyage
Richard Teschner, Austrian, 1879–1948
Color lithograph published by the
Wiener Werkstätte, Vienna

Longingly

1. Ba — by's bed's a sil — ver moon,
2. Ba — by's fish — ing for a dream,

Sail — ing o'er the sky, _____
Fish — ing near and far, _____

Sail — ing o'er the sea of sleep,
Her line a sil — ver moon — beam is,

While the stars float by. _____
Her bait a sil — ver star.

To Refrain after each verse

(Please turn the page.)

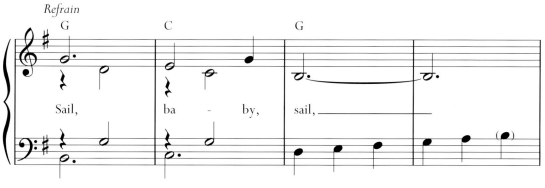

Refrain

Sail, ba - by, sail, _____

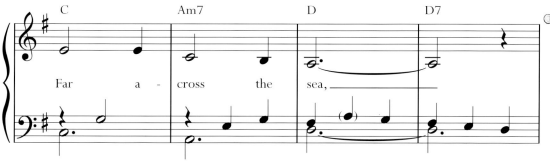

Far a - cross the sea, _____

The Fairy Ship
Illustration by Paul Woodroffe from
Nursery Songs by Joseph Moorat
London, ca. 1907

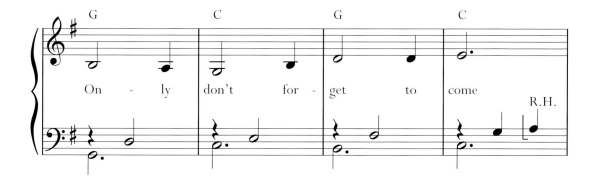

On - ly don't for - get to come
R.H.

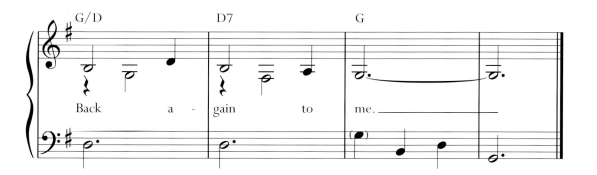

Back a - gain to me. _____

Maternal Caress
Mary Cassatt
American, 1844–1926
Drypoint, aquatint, and soft-ground
etching printed in color; 1890–91

Hand Studies—Child with Doll
Alma Lavenson
American, 1897–1989
Platinum print, 1932

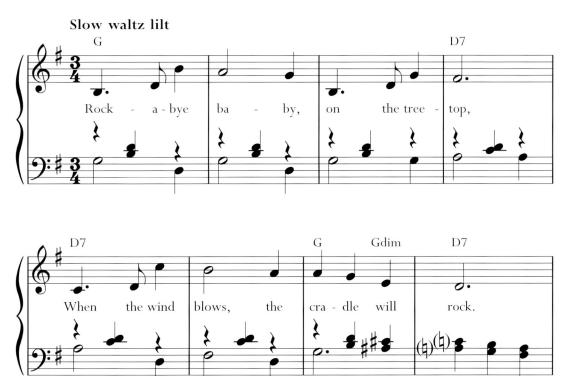

Slow waltz lilt

Rock - a-bye ba - by, on the tree - top,

When the wind blows, the cra - dle will rock.

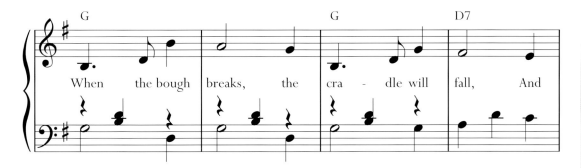

When the bough breaks, the cra - dle will fall, And

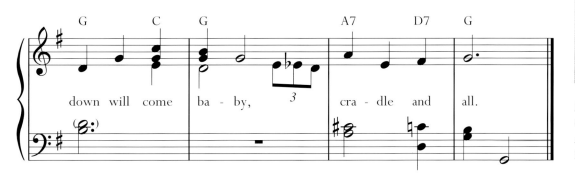

down will come ba - by, cra - dle and all.

Rock-a-Bye, Baby

*The best-known lullaby in
the English language,
it is also probably the first
that children learn themselves,
to sing to their dolls,
stuffed animals, or siblings.*

Blossom Day
Gertrude Käsebier
American, 1852–1934
Platinum print, 1904–1905

Little Boy Blue

Some children can sleep soundly through any amount of commotion. Little Boy Blue of this nursery rhyme was apparently able to continue his nap in spite of the chaos that ensued.

The Grandchildren of Sir William Heathcote (detail)
William Owen
British, 1769–1825
Oil on canvas

The Monet Family in Their Garden at Argenteuil (detail)
Édouard Manet
French, 1832–1883
Oil on canvas

Bluely

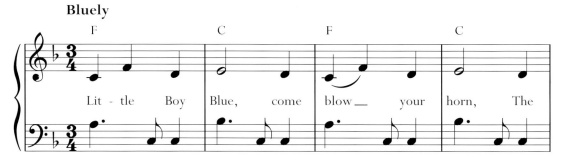

Lit - tle Boy Blue, come blow your horn, The

sheep's in the mead - ow, the cow's in the corn.

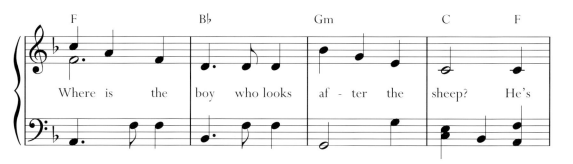

Where is the boy who looks af - ter the sheep? He's

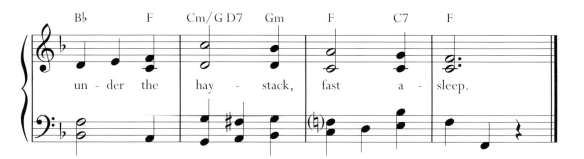

un - der the hay - stack, fast a - sleep.

Baloo, Baleerie

"Go away, tiny fairies" insists this Gaelic song.
The *"ben"* is a small inner room, presumably
where the baby sleeps.

Infant Joy
William Blake
British, 1757–1827
Hand-colored relief etching from
Songs of Innocence, 1789

Ba - loo, ba - leer - ie, ba - loo, ba -

leer - ie, Ba - loo, ba - leer - ie, ba - loo, ba - lee.

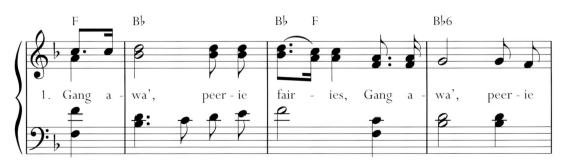

1. Gang a - wa', peer - ie fair - ies, Gang a - wa', peer - ie

fair - ies, Gang a - wa', peer-ie fair - ies, Frae oor ben noo.

Flying Away and *The Fairy Queen Takes an Airy Drive*
Richard Doyle
British, 1824–1883
Chromolithographs from *In Fairyland: A Series of Pictures from the Elf-World*
Published in London by Longmans, Green, Reader and Dyer, 1870

Young Mother
Gazing at Her Child
Adolphe-William
Bouguereau
French, 1825–1905
Oil on canvas

Brezairola (Lullaby)

A folk tune from the Auvergne region of France, this beautiful lullaby expresses the sentiment of many exhausted parents: "Slumber, come quickly!" The lyrics are given in the original dialect, with an English translation following.

Easy lilt

Soun,   soun, bè-ni,   bè-ni, bè-ni;   Soun,   soun, bè-ni,   bè-ni, doun!

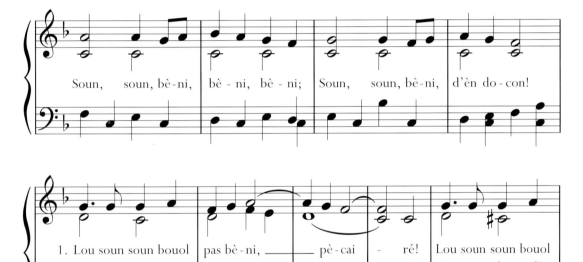

Soun,   soun, bè-ni,   bè-ni, bè-ni;   Soun,   soun, bè-ni,   d'èn do-con!

Shepherd
Detail from *The Nativity*
Antoniazzo Romano (Antonio di
Benedetto Aquilio)
Italian (Roman), active by 1452, d. by 1512
Tempera on wood

1. Lou soun soun bouol   pas bè-ni, _____   pè-cai - ré!   Lou soun soun bouol
2. At - so   lo qu'ès   por o-qui, _____   pè-cai - ré!   At - so   lo qu'ès

2nd time skip to ✆   1st time skip to ℅   ⌢   Fine

pas bè-ni,   Lou nè - ni s'en bouol   pas dur-mi!   Oh!
por o-qui,   Lou né - ni s'en bou - lio dur-mi.   Ah!

(Please turn the page.)

Mother and Child
Mary Cassatt
American, 1844–1926
Pastel on wove paper, mounted on canvas;
1914

Woman Standing, Child on Back (detail)
Jean Charlot
Mexican, 1898–1979
Color lithograph on zinc, 1933

English translation:

Come, slumber, come, come,
Come, slumber, come, please come.
Come, slumber, come, come,
Come, slumber, from where you will.

Slumber does not want to come,
   poor baby.
Slumber does not want to come;
Baby cannot fall asleep. Oh!

Come, come, slumber, come quickly!
Come, come, slumber, come down now!
Slumber does not want to come.
Baby does not want to sleep.

Come, come, slumber, come quickly!
Come, come, come to my
   sweet babe!
Slumber does not want to come.
Baby does not want to sleep.

Come, slumber, come, come,
Come, slumber, come, please come.
Come, slumber, come, come,
Come, slumber, from where you will.

Slumber comes, at last it's here, poor baby.
Slumber comes, at last it's here;
Now the baby will fall asleep. Ah!

Kumbayah

This West Indian song calls out with longing, yet with hope, imploring the Lord to "come by here."

Slowly, with nobility

Refrain

Kum-ba - yah, my Lord, Kum-ba - yah, Kum-ba -

yah, my Lord, Kum-ba - yah, Kum-ba -

yah, my Lord, Kum-ba - yah, Oh,

to Verses • at End

Fine

lord, ___ Kum-ba - yah. (1.—3.) Some-one's yah.

The Goddess Isis with Her Son Horus on Her Lap
Egyptian, Ptolemaic Period (305–30 B.C.)
Blue faience

cry - ing,
sing - ing, Lord,   Kum - ba - yah,   Some-one's
sleep - ing,

cry - ing,
sing - ing, Lord,   Kum - ba - yah,   Some-one's
sleep - ing,

cry - ing,
sing - ing, Lord,   Kum - ba - yah,   Oh,
sleep - ing,

Lord, _____   Kum - ba - yah.

Drum
African, Republic of the Congo,
Vili or Yombe people, 19th century
Wood, carved and painted glass

Raindrops

The gentle drumming of rain on the roof can have the mesmeric effect of a lullaby.

With a slow, rocking pulse

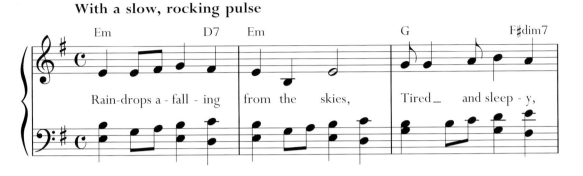

Rain-drops a - fall - ing | from the skies, | Tired_ and sleep - y,

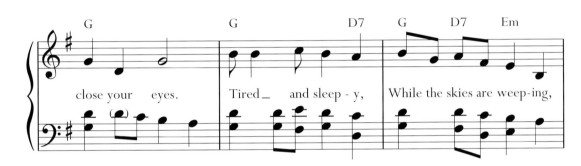

close your eyes. | Tired_ and sleep - y, | While the skies are weep-ing,

Weep-ing and sing-ing you their | lul - la - bies. | Tired_ and sleep-y,

While the skies are weep-ing, | Weep-ing and sing-ing you their | lul - la - bies.

Mother's Kiss
Mary Cassatt
American, 1844–1926
Drypoint and aquatint printed in color,
ca. 1890–91

Seidō and Kanda River from Shōhei Bridge
(detail)
Utagawa Hiroshige
Japanese, 1797–1858
Woodblock print in colors from the series
One Hundred Famous Views of Edo, 1857

73

Sweet and Low

Alfred, Lord Tennyson (1809–1892),
Poet Laureate of England, wrote this poem,
which recounts the words of a woman
longing for her husband to return safely
from the sea. The melody is by Sir Joseph
Barnby (1838–1896).

Slow waltz

C   F   G7   C

Sweet   and   low,   sweet   and   low,

Cm   D7   Dsus   G

Wind   of   the   west - ern   sea, ____

Sailing Ship (detail)
H. M. Lawrence
American, 19th century
Color lithograph poster for *The Century,*
October 1895

C   Cdim   Em   Am

Low,   low,   breathe and   blow, _____

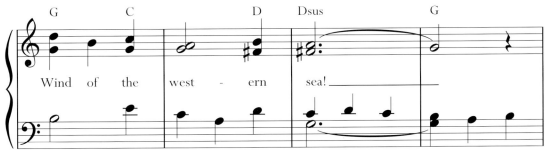

G   C   D   Dsus   G

Wind of the   west - ern   sea! _____

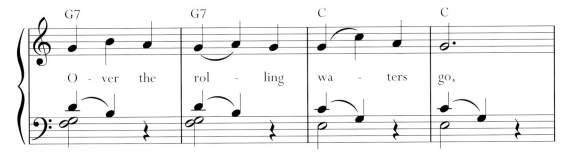

G7   G7   C   C

O - ver the   rol - ling   wa - ters go,

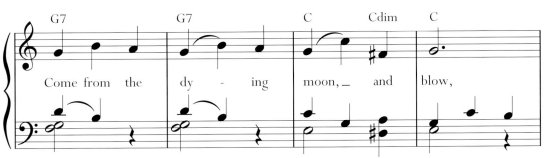

G7   G7   C   Cdim   C

Come from the   dy - ing   moon, _ and   blow,

(Please turn the page.)

Baby Monsarrat
Clarence H. White
American, 1871–1925
Platinum print, 1905

Sweet and Low continued

Family Group
Henry Moore
British, 1898–1986
Bronze, 1944

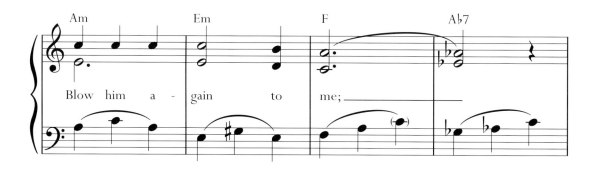

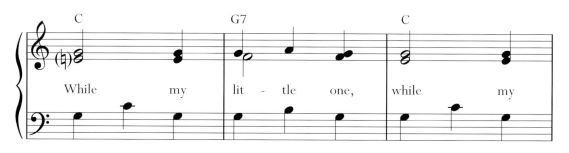

Additional verse:

2. Sleep and rest, sleep and rest,
   Father will come to thee soon;
   Rest, rest, on mother's breast,
   Father will come to thee soon;
   Father will come to his babe in the nest,
   Silver sails all out of the west
   Under the silver moon;
   Sleep, my little one, sleep, my pretty one, sleep.

The Dock
B. J. O. Norfeldt
American, 1878–1955
Color woodblock print

Two Girls, One Holding a Baby
Édouard Vuillard
French, 1868–1940
Color lithograph

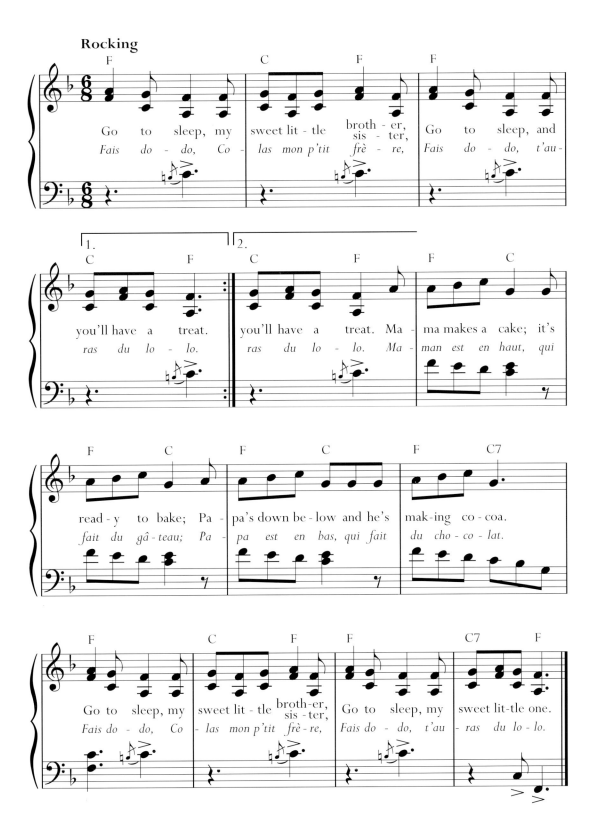

Fais Dodo (Go to Sleep)

As you sing this old French song, you can change "brother" to "sister," "nephew," "grandchild," "baby," or whatever name is appropriate.

Rocking

Go to sleep, my | sweet lit-tle broth-er, sis-ter, | Go to sleep, and
Fais do-do, Co- | las mon p'tit frè-re, | Fais do-do, t'au-

1. you'll have a treat.
ras du lo-lo.

2. you'll have a treat. Ma- | ma makes a cake; it's
ras du lo-lo. Ma- | man est en haut, qui

read-y to bake; Pa- | pa's down be-low and he's | mak-ing co-coa.
fait du gâ-teau; Pa- | pa est en bas, qui fait | du cho-co-lat.

Go to sleep, my | sweet lit-tle broth-er, sis-ter, | Go to sleep, my | sweet lit-tle one.
Fais do-do, Co- | las mon p'tit frè-re, | Fais do-do, t'au- | ras du lo-lo.

Fais Dodo, Colas
Maurice Boutet de Monvel
French, 1851–1913
Illustration from *Vieilles chansons et rondes pour les petits enfants*
Published in Paris

Toora, Loora, Loora

Slow waltz

Too - ra, loo - ra, loo - ra,

Too - ra, loo - ra - li,

Too - ra, loo - ra, loo - ra,

Hush, now, don't you cry. Ah,

(Please turn the page.)

Though mostly nonsense syllables, this song by James R. Shannon seems to express a longing for the writer's homeland and childhood.

Family Group
Gertrude Käsebier, American, 1852–1934
Platinum print, 1902

Nurse and Child (detail)
Mary Cassatt, American, 1844–1926
Pastel on colored wove paper, mounted on canvas; 1897

A Nanny with Her Charge
Maurice Prendergast
American, 1858–1924
Watercolor on paper from
the *Large Boston Public Garden
Sketchbook,* 1895–97

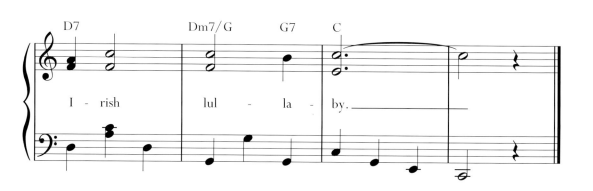

Bye, Baby Bunting

Although the origin of the word "bunting" is unclear, it has come to mean a baby's snuggly, hooded sleeper or outer wrapper.

Baby's Bassinet
Illustration from *Le Journal de Bébé* by Marie Madeleine Franc-Nohain Published by Bernard Grasset, Paris, 1914

Gently swinging

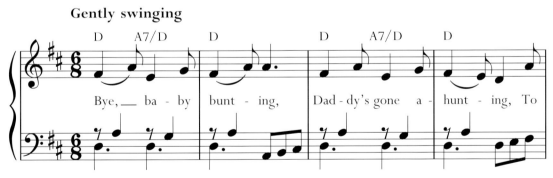

Bye, — ba - by bunt - ing, Dad - dy's gone a - hunt - ing, To

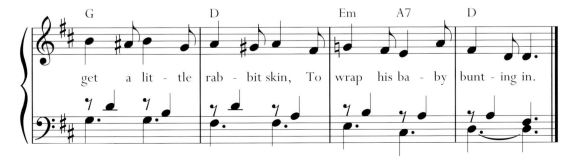

get a lit - tle rab - bit skin, To wrap his ba - by bunt - ing in.

Twinkle, Twinkle, Little Star

These familiar lyrics first appeared in Rhymes for the Nursery *by Jane and Ann Taylor,* published in England in 1806. They were later set to a traditional tune to create this beloved children's song.

Slow and twinkling

1. Twin-kle, twin-kle, lit - tle star,
2. When the blaz-ing sun is gone,

How I won-der what you are!
When he noth-ing shines up - on,

Up a-bove the world so high,
Then you show your lit - tle light,

Like a dia-mond in the sky.
Twin-kle, twin-kle, all the night.

Twin-kle, twin-kle, lit - tle star,
Twin-kle, twin-kle, lit - tle star,

How I won-der what you are!
How I won-der what you are!

Portrait of a Child (Clara B. Fuller)
Lucia Fairchild Fuller
American, 1872–1924
Watercolor on ivory, 1898

The Way Home
Ludwig Michaelek
Austrian, 1859–1942
Color etching and aquatint, 1901

Additional verses:

3. Then the trav'ler in the dark
   Thanks you for your tiny spark;
   He could not see which way to go,
   If you did not twinkle so.
   Twinkle, twinkle, little star,
   How I wonder what you are!

4. In the dark blue sky you keep,
   Often through my curtains peep,
   For you never shut your eye,
   Till the sun is in the sky,
   Twinkle, twinkle, little star,
   How I wonder what you are!

INDEX OF FIRST LINES

All night, all day	91
Baby's bed's a silver moon	56
Baloo, baleerie, baloo, baleerie	64
Bye, baby bunting, Daddy's gone a-hunting	83
By'm bye, by'm bye	53
Dance, little baby, dance up high	20
Dance to your daddy, my little baby	11
Day is done, gone the sun	49
Go to sleep, my sweet little brother	79
Golden slumbers kiss your eyes	44
Good night to you all, and sweet be your sleep	92
Hush, little baby, don't say a word	8
Hush-a-bye, don't you cry	15
Kumbayah, my Lord, Kumbayah	70
Little baby, sweetly sleep, do not weep	54
Little Boy Blue, come blow your horn	62
Lullaby and goodnight, with roses bedight	23
Mammy loves and Pappy loves	17
Matthew, Mark, Luke, and John	89
Now the day is over	13
Oh, can ye sew cushions, and can ye sew sheets	31
Raindrops a-falling from the skies	73
Rock-a-bye, baby, on the treetop	61
Skidamarink a-dink a-dink, skidamarink a-doo	47
Sleep, baby, sleep, your father tends the sheep	18
Sleep, little one, go to sleep	34
Sleep, my baby, on my bosom	50
Sleep, my child, and peace attend thee	41
Sleep, my little one, my loved one	27
Soun, soun, bèni, bèni, bèni (Come, slumber, come, come)	67
Sweet and low, sweet and low	74
Swing low, sweet chariot	28
The Sandman comes	37
To my little one's cradle in the night	38
Toora, loora, loora	81
Twinkle, twinkle, little star	84
When at night I go to sleep	87

CREDITS

Page 9: Gift of Frederic H. Hatch, 1926   26.97. *Page 10:* Gift of George N. and Helen M. Richard, 1964   64.165.2. *Page 11:* Robert Lehman Collection, 1975   1975.1.231. *Page 12:* Purchase, Mrs. Vincent Astor and Mrs. Charles S. Payson Gifts and Harris Brisbane Dick and Rogers Funds, 1972   1972.133.2. *Page 13:* Bequest of Robert Graham Dun, 1911   11.45.3. *Page 14:* From the Collection of James Stillman, Gift of Dr. Ernest G. Stillman, 1922   22.16.21. *Page 15:* The Glenn Tilley Morse Collection, Bequest of Glenn Tilley Morse, 1950   50.602.565. *Page 16:* top, Gift of Countess Bismarck, 1961   61.259; bottom, Museum Accession, 1943. *Page 17:* Gift of Edgar William and Bernice Chrysler Garbisch, 1972   1972.263.6. *Page 18:* Museum Accession, 1943. *Page 19:* Gift of Mrs. J. Insley Blair, 1950   50.228.3. *Page 20:* Rogers Fund, 1947   47.70. *Page 21:* Alfred Stieglitz Collection, 1933   33.43.27. *Page 22:* Charles Stewart Smith Collection, Gift of Mrs. Charles Stewart Smith, Charles Stewart Smith Jr. and Howard Caswell Smith, in memory of Charles Stewart Smith, 1914   14.76.70f. *Page 23:* Gift of Mrs. John LaPorte Given, 1945   45.110.4. *Page 24:* Rogers Fund, 1943   43.11.4. *Page 25:* Bequest of Francis T. S. Darley, 1914   14.126.6. *Page 26:* The Harry G. C. Packard Collection of Asian Art, Gift of Harry G. C. Packard and Purchase, Fletcher, Rogers, Harris Brisbane Dick and Louis V. Bell Funds, Joseph Pulitzer Bequest and The Annenberg Fund Inc. Gift, 1975   1975.268.137. *Page 27:* H. O. Havemeyer Collection, Bequest of Mrs. H. O. Havemeyer, 1929   29.107.97. *Page 28:* Friends of the American Wing Fund, 1966   66.10.23. *Page 29:* Gift of Mr. and Mrs. Samuel Shore, 1978   1978.61.2. *Page 30:* Gift of Mrs. B. J. O. Norfeldt, 1955   55.634.79. *Page 31:* Gift of the artist, 1960   60.713.40. *Page 32:* Gift of Mrs. Adolf Obrig, in memory of her husband, 1917   17.138.2. *Page 33:* The Friedsam Collection, Bequest of Michael Friedsam, 1931   32.100.5. *Page 34:* Gift of Geraldine C. Herzfeld, in memory of her husband, Monroe Eliot Hemmerdinger, 1984   1984.34. *Page 35:* Catharine Lorillard Wolfe Collection, Bequest of Catharine Lorillard Wolfe, 1887   87.15.8. *Page 36:* top, Robert Lehman Collection, 1975   1975.1.727b; bottom, Mary Martin Fund, 1987   1987.1117. *Page 37:* Rogers Fund, 1922   JP1278. *Page 38:* Alfred Stieglitz Collection, 1933   33.43.235 *Page 39:* Bequest of Scofield Thayer, 1982   1984.433.2. *Page 40:* Alfred Stieglitz Collection, 1949   49.55.287. *Page 41:* Gift of Alice Boney, 1954   54.37.2. *Page 42:* Gift of Alexander Smith Cochran, 1913   13.228.28. *Page 43:* Rogers Fund, 1970   1970.217. *Page 44:* Gift of Mrs. Paul Moore, 1938   38.72. *Page 45:* Rogers Fund, 1947   47.127.3. *Page 46:* Bequest of Arthur M. Bullowa, 1993   1993.406.2. *Page 47:* Rogers Fund, 1919   JP1123. *Page 48:* Rogers Fund, 1922   22.82.1(3). *Page 49:* Sansbury-Mills Fund, 1961   61.47.3. *Page 50:* H. O. Havemeyer Collection, Bequest of Mrs. H. O. Havemeyer, 1929   29.100.50. *Page 51:* H. O. Havemeyer Collection, Gift of Mrs. P. H. B. Frelinghuysen, 1930   30.13. *Page 52:* Robert Lehman Collection, 1975   1975.1.592. *Page 53:* Fletcher Fund, 1937   37.176.3. *Page 54:* The Michael C. Rockefeller Memorial Collection, Bequest of Nelson A. Rockefeller, 1979   1979.206.1440. *Page 55:* H. O. Havemeyer Collection, Bequest of Mrs. H. O. Havemeyer, 1929   JP1671. *Page 56:* Museum Accession, 1943. *Page 57:* Robert Lehman Collection, 1975   1975.1.953. *Page 58:* Gift of Paul J. Sachs, 1916   16.2.5. *Page 59:* Museum Accession, 1984   1984.1056.24. *Page 60:* Stewart S. MacDermott Fund, 1987   1987.1035. *Page 61:* Alfred Stieglitz Collection, 1933   33.43.135. *Page 62:* Gift of the Heathcote Art Foundation, 1986   1986.264.4. *Page 63:* Bequest of Joan Whitney Payson, 1975   1976.201.14. *Page 64:* top, Gift of Lincoln Kirstein, 1970   1970.565.74; bottom, Rogers Fund, 1917   17.10.25. *Page 65:* Gift of Lincoln Kirstein, 1970   1970.565.74. *Page 66:* Bequest of Zene Montgomery Pyle, 1993   1993.402. *Page 67:* Rogers Fund, 1906   06.1214. *Page 68:* H. O. Havemeyer Collection, Bequest of Mrs. H. O. Havemeyer, 1929   29.100.49. *Page 69:* Gift of the artist, 1960   60.713.42. *Page 70:* Purchase, Joseph Pulitzer Bequest, 1955   55.121.5. *Page 71:* The Crosby Brown Collection of Musical Instruments, 1889   89.4.1743. *Page 72:* The Howard Mansfield Collection, Purchase, Rogers Fund, 1936   JP2512. *Page 73:* Gift of Paul J. Sachs, 1916   16.2.10. *Page 74:* Leonard A. Lauder Collection of American Posters, Gift of Leonard A. Lauder, 1984   1984.1202.57. *Page 75:* Alfred Stieglitz Collection, 1933   33.43.316. *Page 76:* Anonymous Gift, in honor of Alfred H. Barr Jr., 1981   1981.488.4. *Page 77:* Gift of Mrs. B. J. O. Norfeldt, 1955   55.634.80. *Page 78:* Harris Brisbane Dick Fund, 1925   25.70.25. *Page 79:* Gift of Mrs. John S. Lamont, 1974   1974.669. *Page 80:* Gift of Mrs. Ralph J. Hines, 1960   60.181. *Page 81:* Alfred Stieglitz Collection, 1933   33.43.370. *Page 82:* Robert Lehman Collection, 1975   1975.1.942. *Page 83:* The Elisha Whittelsey Collection, The Elisha Whittelsey Fund, 1977   1977.588.1. *Page 84:* Rogers Fund, 1914   14.57.3. *Page 85:* Rogers Fund, 1923   23.52.12(4). *Page 86:* Maria DeWitt Jesup Fund, 1965   65.49. *Page 87:* Robert Lehman Collection, 1975   1975.1.71. *Page 88:* Gift of Ruth Blumka, in memory of Leopold Blumka, 1974   1974.121. *Page 89:* Rogers Fund, 1921   21.36.91. *Page 90:* Bequest of Jane Kendall Gingrich, 1982   1982.55.3. *Page 91:* Purchase, Mrs. Roger Brunschwig Gift, 1988   1988.24.1. *Page 92:* Gift of Miss Adelaide Milton de Groot, in memory of the de Groot and Hawley Families, 1966   66.167.

INDEX OF SONG TITLES

All Night, All Day	90	Little Boy Blue	62
All the Pretty Little Horses	14	Mammy Loves	17
All Through the Night	40	Matthew, Mark, Luke, and John	89
Armenian Lullaby	26	Mozart's Lullaby	34
Baby's Bed's a Silver Moon	56	Now the Day Is Over	12
Baloo, Baleerie	64	Raindrops	72
Brahms' Lullaby	23	Raisins and Almonds	38
Brezairola (Lullaby)	66	Rock-a-Bye, Baby	60
Bye, Baby Bunting	83	Rocking	54
By'm Bye	52	The Sandman	37
Can Ye Sew Cushions	30	Skidamarink	46
Dance, Little Baby	20	Sleep, Baby, Sleep	18
Dance to Your Daddy	10	Suo Gan (Lullaby)	50
Day Is Done	49	Sweet and Low	74
Fais Dodo (Go to Sleep)	78	Swing Low, Sweet Chariot	28
Golden Slumbers	44	Toora, Loora, Loora	80
Good Night to You All	92	Twinkle, Twinkle, Little Star	84
Hush, Little Baby	8	When at Night I Go to Sleep	86
Kumbayah	70		

Good Night to You All

A musical family might sing this round to one another at bedtime.

*Virgin and Child with the Young
Saint John the Baptist and Angels*
François Boucher
French, 1703–1770
Oil on canvas, 1765

To be sung as a round, voices entering at I, II, and III

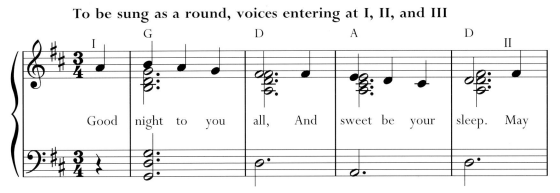

Good night to you all, And sweet be your sleep. May

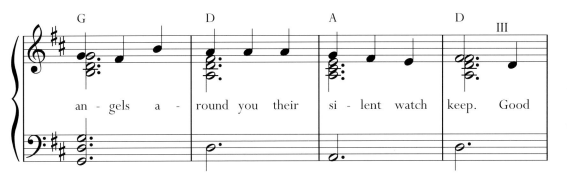

an - gels a - round you their si - lent watch keep. Good

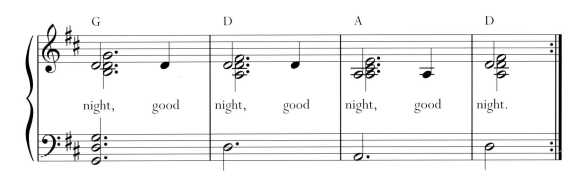

night, good night, good night, good night.

All Night, All Day

It's a cheering thought to imagine that angels are watching over our children day and night.

Fan Quilt
United States, ca. 1900
Cotton

With spirit

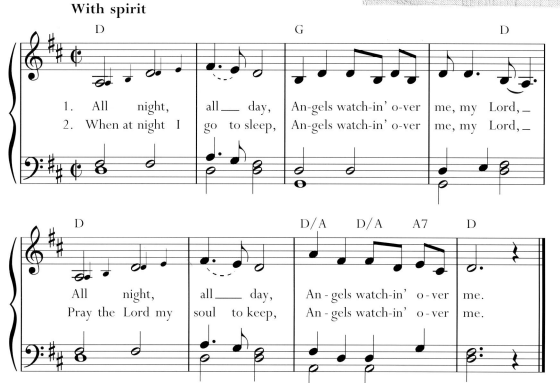

1. All night, all ___ day, An-gels watch-in' o-ver me, my Lord, ___
2. When at night I go to sleep, An-gels watch-in' o-ver me, my Lord, ___

All night, all ___ day, An - gels watch-in' o-ver me.
Pray the Lord my soul to keep, An - gels watch-in' o-ver me.

Asleep
Horace Pippin
American, 1888–1946
Oil on canvas board, 1943

90

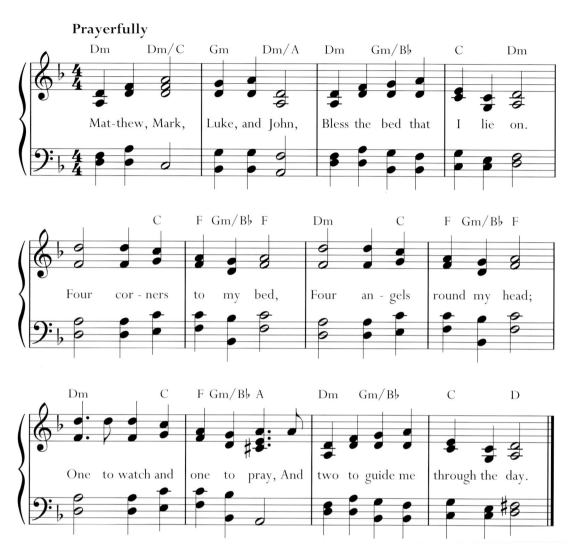

Prayerfully

Mat-thew, Mark, Luke, and John, Bless the bed that I lie on.

Four cor-ners to my bed, Four an-gels round my head;

One to watch and one to pray, And two to guide me through the day.

Matthew, Mark, Luke, and John

A traditional nursery prayer, this verse seems almost a spell or incantation to protect the bed of the sleeping child.

Waking
Detail from *A Day in a Child's Life*
Hand-colored wood engraving after a
drawing by Kate Greenaway
(British, 1846–1901), 1881

Two who warm-ly cov — er, Two who o'er me hov — er,

Two to whom 'tis giv — en To guide my steps to heav — en.

Crib of the Infant Jesus
South Netherlandish, Brabant,
15th century
Wood, polychromed and gilt,
lead, silver gilt, painted
parchment, and silk embroidery
with seed pearls, gold thread,
and translucent enamels

When at Night I Go to Sleep

Engelbert Humperdinck (1854–1921) based the evening prayer for his
opera Hansel and Gretel on the German version of "Now I Lay Me Down
to Sleep." It is closely related to "Matthew, Mark, Luke, and John."

Calmly

When at night I go to sleep, Four-teen an-gels watch do keep;

Two my head are guard - ing, Two my feet are guid - ing, —

Two are on my right hand, — Two are on my left hand,

(Please turn the page.)

The Archangel Raphael and Tobias
Neri di Bicci
Italian (Florentine), 1419–1491
Tempera on panel

Ernesta (Child with Nurse) (detail)
Cecilia Beaux
American, 1855–1942
Oil on canvas, 1894